GROWN-UP FAITH

KEVIN MYERS
WITH CHARLIE WETZEL

PARTICIPANT WORKBOOK

Copyright © 2019 by Leadership Gravity, LLC, and Wetzel & Wetzel, LLC

ALL RIGHTS RESERVED

Published by Lifetogether Ministries

Copyright retained by Leadership Gravity, LLC, Wetzel $ Wetzel, LLC.

Use of this curriculum template is retained by Lifetogether Ministires.

Scripture quotations marked (MSG) are taken from THE MESSAGE: Copyright © 1993, 1994, 1995, 1996, 2000, 2001, 2002, 2005. Used by permission of NavPress Publishing Group.

Scripture quotations marked (NIV2011) are taken from the HOLY BIBLE, NEW INTERNATIONAL VERSION®. Copyright 1973, 1978, 1984 and 2011 by Biblica, Inc.® Used by permission. All rights reserved worldwide.

ISBN: 978-1-950007-20-2
Printed in the United States of America

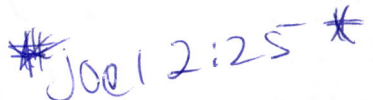

TABLE OF CONTENTS

Introduction by Kevin Myers   4
Endorsements   6
Using This Workbook (Read This First)   10
Outline for Each Session   12

Session One: Foundations   14
Session Two: God's Bigger Picture   24
Session Three: It's Time to Train   34
Session Four: Engaging the Heart   44
Session Five: The Freedom of Obedience   54
Session Six: Living God's Bigger Life   64

INTRODUCTION

WELCOME!

Most people have bits and pieces of the Bible, but they are puzzled about the whole. In truth, most have never heard a simple yet meaningful way to understand the Bible. And further, they don't know the 10 core questions of life nor how to engage them. For example:

Is life an accident or am I here on purpose?

Why do bad things happen to good people?

Why can't God just accept me as I am?

What does it mean to be forgiven?

Are heaven and hell real?

And that's why we wrote the small group material to accompany the book, *Grown Up Faith: God's Big Picture for a Bigger Life*. We hope it does for you what it did for Ernie Johnson and his wife Cheryl:

"I was as far away from God as you can possibly imagine.

You know what the game changer was? It was the teaching that you'll find in the book, "Grown Up Faith: God's Big Picture for a Bigger Life". Some years back, Kevin would visit with me and my wife Cheryl, who was, I might add, equally distant from God at that time. The meetings took place in our home, and there, across the kitchen table or sitting in the den, Kevin walked us through the Bible.

For so long I had considered that dust-covered, unused wedding gift which sat in the corner of the attic to be antiquated, out of touch, irrelevant in this modern time. But in those weeks, the Bible became something new, something fresh... my roadmap, a source of strength. Whether you've been around church your entire life or spent a good bit of time wandering in the desert like I did, you will find this book fascinating and encouraging, and its message timeless. It may take you places you would have never seen yourself going. I'm talking about becoming the spouse, the parent, the leader that you were created to be. That's what happens when you put your mind, your heart, and your soul into having a grown-up faith."

Ernie Johnson, Jr. Sportscaster, TNT and author of *Unscripted: The Unpredictable Moments that Make Life Extraordinary*

Grown Up Faith was originally a tool to disciple my kids and transform people in our territory. Now it's a book along with this small group material so that you can experience what Ernie and Cheryl did years ago. Once you see it, you'll never be the same. Welcome to the journey!

KEVIN MYERS
12Stone Church, Founding Pastor

ENDORSEMENTS

PRAISE FOR GROWN-UP FAITH

For about the last 30 years, I've been a national television sportscaster, and on more than one occasion I've asked myself, "How did I get here?" Not on this planet, but in front of a thousand realtors at a prayer breakfast talking about my faith in Jesus Christ, or at midfield of the Mercedes Benz Stadium delivering the invocation before an NCAA football game.

I guess the question kept coming to mind because if you had known me in my college days and into the early years of my professional career, and were voting on the least likely man to give the keynote at a prayer breakfast - I would have won by a landslide. I was as far away from God as you can possibly imagine. You know what the game changer was? It was the teaching you'll find in this book.

Grown-up Faith: God's Big Picture for a Bigger Life was written by my pastor, Kevin Myers. In the fall and winter of 1997, Kevin would visit with me and my wife Cheryl, who was, I might add, equally distant from God at the time. The meetings took place in our home. There, across the kitchen table or sitting in the den, Kevin walked us through the Bible.

For so long I had considered that dust-covered, unused wedding gift, which sat in the corner of the attic, to be antiquated, out of touch, irrelevant in this modern time. But in those weeks and months of questioning and wrestling, the Bible became something new, something fresh. Kevin allowed me to see it in an entirely new light, and it became my road map, a source of comfort and strength. I remember Kevin describing it this way: the Bible isn't a history book; it's a love letter from God to His people.

Whether you've been around church your entire life or spent a good bit of time wandering in the desert like I did, you will find this book fascinating and encouraging, and its message timeless. It may take you places you would have never seen yourself going. I'm not talking about speaking engagements and invocations; I'm talking about becoming the spouse, the parent, the leader that you were created to be. That's what happens when

you put your mind, your heart, and your soul into having a grown-up faith.
As you read, be prepared to have your eyes opened to a magnificent teaching. (I'd have a box of highlighters handy, too.)

Ernie Johnson Jr., sportscaster, TNT, and author of *Unscripted: The Unpredictable Moments That Make Life Extraordinary*

As followers of Jesus, we often talk a lot about growing in our faith. What's often not discussed, however, is what true spiritual maturity looks like. In Grown-up Faith, Kevin Myers reveals how we can become more like Jesus, bearing fruit as we blossom in the fullness of the abundant life Christ promises us. Thorough and thoughtful, biblical and practical, this book provides a road map for us as we measure each milestone in the journey of our faith.

Chris Hodges, senior pastor, Church of the Highlands, and author of *The Daniel Dilemma* and *What's Next?*

A book in a class all by itself. This is not just one more discipleship book. It explodes with the invitation and opportunities God has for people who start on the journey of faith with Him, and compellingly gives the pathway to move forward and live out God's purposes beyond imagination. No sugarcoating, no pie in the sky. Reading it I was immersed in the presence of God—and Oh!—the last chapter makes "Living Sent" urgent! Read alone, or read with a group—God will be present.

Jo Anne Lyon, ambassador and general superintendent emerita,
The Wesleyan Church

This is what I like about my friend Kevin Myers: he challenges me, makes the complicated simple, and gives me pragmatic ways to get unstuck in my faith journey. I came to Christian faith as a young boy of seven, and almost six decades later, I'm still trying to grow up. In "*Grown-up Faith*", Kevin helps me align my mind, heart, and will to actualize abundant life as promised by our Lord. You, too, will find this book excitingly encouraging. Thanks, Kevin, for helping me grow.

Sam Chand, leadership consultant and author of *Leadership Pain* (www.samchand.com)

Kevin Myers has a track record of getting people to a new place. I found this book helpful in better understanding some of the tensions that trip us up as we head to a new place spiritually. This book will be very helpful for anyone who wants more than they have now.

Brian Tome, senior pastor, Crossroads Church, Cincinnati, Ohio

This book will touch your heart, make you think, and empower your choices for a life full of what matters and lasts. The big story of God and the Bible is intertwined with loads of personal stories Kevin shares with great transparency and humor. Whether just investigating faith or on a lifelong journey, you'll be inspired with fresh insights into life's great questions.

Dr. Wayne Schmidt, general superintendent, The Wesleyan Church

Everyone desires to know their role in the big picture, but the big questions that give clarity are intimidating. In this much-needed book, Kevin Myers provides more than the answers. He explains the big picture and guides his readers on the path to discovering a faith that will allow them to be who they were created to be.

Ken Coleman, host of *The Ken Coleman Show* and author of *The Proximity Principle*

USING THIS WORKBOOK

TOOLS TO HELP YOU HAVE A GREAT SMALL GROUP EXPERIENCE!

1.

Use this workbook as a guide, not a straightjacket. If the group responds to the lesson in an unexpected but honest way, go with that. If you think of a better question than the next one in the lesson, ask it. The goal of the group is to engage in practical conversation.

2.

Enjoy your small group experience and have fun! Be honest and open in the conversations and make the most of your time together.

3.

Pray before each session—for your group members, for your discussion, and for wisdom and fresh perspective.

4.

Read the outline for each session on the next pages so that you understand how the sessions will flow.

OUTLINE OF EACH SESSION

Read through this outline to get a clear idea of how each group meeting will be structured. A typical group session for the *"Grown Up Faith"* study will include the following sections.

INTRODUCTION. Each lesson opens with a brief thought that will help you prepare for the session and get you thinking about the particular subject you will explore with your group. You will want to have the group read them aloud together to begin each session. This section includes some simple questions to get you talking—letting you share as much or as little as you feel comfortable doing.

WEEKLY SCRIPTURE. Each will focus on a scripture that emphasizes an important truth from the session. Take the time to read it aloud as a group, and even consider memorizing it as a great way to engage in the study.

WATCH VIDEO SESSION. As a group, you'll watch the teaching together. As you watch, your focus shouldn't be on simply accumulating information. Rather, focus on how you should live and what you should do in light of the content and scripture. We want to help you apply the insights practically and creatively, from your heart as well as your head. At the end of the day, allowing the timeless truths from God's Word to transform our lives in Christ should be your greatest aim.

NOTES. Each session, take the time to take notes as you watch the teaching video. It could be as simple as a key phrase or statement that resonates with you, or a larger big idea that you want to discuss together as a group. Either way, this engagement during the video session will aid in your group discussion and practical application.

GROUP DISCUSSION. Here, your group will have the opportunity to respond to the video content. Spiritual growth happens best when we truly internalize and discuss the content with the goal of application. Pursuing an intimate connection with God and His family is key for the growth to take place. This section includes opportunities to review the video, discuss some simple questions, and pose larger, foundational faith topics. Each session's discussion section aims to establish greater understanding, deeper group connections and overall encouragement in your spiritual journey. You will find some suggested group questions in this booklet that may help guide this discussion time, but don't feel restrained or limited to these questions.

TAKE ACTION. God wants you to be a part of His Kingdom—to weave your story into His. That will mean change. It will require you to go His way rather than your own. This won't happen overnight, but it should happen steadily. By making small, simple choices to act, we can begin to change our direction. This is where the Bible's instructions to "be doers of the Word, not just hearers" (James 1:22) comes into play. Many people skip over this aspect of the Christian life because it's scary, relationally awkward, or simply too much work for their busy schedules. But Jesus wanted all of His disciples to know Him personally, carry out His commands, and help outsiders connect with Him. In this study, you'll have an opportunity to go beyond just Bible study to biblical living. This section will also have a question or two that will challenge you to take action by serving others, sharing your faith, and taking ownership of your personal faith journey.

FOR ADDITIONAL STUDY. If you have time and want to dig deeper into the topic, we'll suggest either Bible passages or chapters of the *"Grown Up Faith"* book that relate to the topic at hand. The group may choose to read and prepare before each meeting in order to cover more material, or group members can use the additional study section during the week for personal study.

DAILY DEVOTIONS. Each week on the Daily Devotions pages, we provide scriptures to read and reflect on between sessions. This provides you with a chance to slow down, read just a small portion of scripture each day, and reflect and pray through it. You'll then have a chance to journal your response to what you've read. Use this section to seek God on your own throughout the week. This time at home should begin and end with prayer. Don't get in a hurry; take enough time to hear God's voice.

1

FOUNDATIONS

INTRODUCTION:

Growing up in the faith, or "Spiritual Maturity", develops as we practically engage with God in three distinct areas: our heart, our mind, and our will. But growing up first requires a strong foundation. Our life will never be stronger than our foundation, and we'll often find ourselves stuck in our faith when we lack what it takes to develop maturity. Today we'll dive into the basics of what it takes to become a grown-up believer and explore God's bigger picture for a bigger life.

ICE-BREAKERS:

Have everyone introduce themselves and answer these questions: What brought you here? What do you hope to get out of this group?

Since we're calling this study *"Grown Up Faith,"* let's talk a little about maturity.

In high school, were you the playful, class clown or the serious, responsible type? Share a story that illustrates.

How does the world define "growing up?" What do you think it takes to be considered a grown-up?

WEEKLY SCRIPTURE:

Therefore everyone who hears these words of mine and puts them into practice is like a wise man who built his house on the rock.
(Matthew 7:24 NIV)

Like the foundations of the house you live in, the foundations of life are not always obvious or visible. But over time, they determine the ultimate strength, stability, and success of what you are trying to build. The foundation determines whether the structure built will stand or fall. That's why we begin this series with a conversation about the foundation for our own life.

WATCH THE

VIDEO

SESSION 1

Use the Notes space provided to record key thoughts, questions, and things you want to remember or come back to as a group. After watching the video, follow along with the questions and scriptures in the Group Discussion section.

GROUP DISCUSSION

Read Matthew 7:24-27 (MSG)

"These words I speak to you are not incidental additions to your life, homeowner improvements to your standard of living. They are foundational words, words to build a life on. If you work these words into your life, you are like a smart carpenter who built his house on solid rock. Rain poured down, the river flooded, a tornado hit—but nothing moved that house. It was fixed to the rock. But if you just use my words in Bible studies and don't work them into your life, you are like a stupid carpenter who built his house on the sandy beach. When a storm rolled in and the waves came up, it collapsed like a house of cards."

In Jesus' parable, what do the two life-builders have in common and how are they different?

Once the two houses are built, what happens to each of them? What do you think Jesus is saying about the different approaches to building the houses?

Based on the video and Jesus' parable, what is the strongest and longest-lasting foundation for living?

- What do you believe "rain, the floods, and the tornados" represent? What do these look like in real life?

- Share a time when you experienced a "storm" in your life and/or when your foundation was tested?

This passage in Matthew was Jesus' wrap-up of a longer teaching we call "The Sermon on the Mount", where he repeatedly invited His listeners to apply what He was saying to their personal lives. Here, He insists on the big picture application, dividing His audience into two groups. They have all heard, but they will make one of two choices about what they have heard: **Build your foundation on Solid Rock or Sandy Beach.** It doesn't matter how good the house looks and even how well it's built if the foundation underneath is questionable. The challenges of life were the same for both houses. The well-built house wasn't immune to storms. But the different foundations led to different outcomes when the winds and waves attacked.

If you had to describe the current foundation of your life, what terms would you use and why?

Pastor Kevin referenced the "10 Core Questions of Life" as foundational. From the list below, which of these would you say challenges your foundation, or tests your faith the most?

- 1. Is life an accident or am I here on purpose?
- 2. Why do bad things happen to good people?
- 3. Can I really trust God?
- 4. Why can't I make my own rules?
- 5. Why can't God just accept me as I am?
- 6. Isn't one way to God narrow-minded?
- 7. What does it mean to be forgiven?
- 8. Why don't Christians look different from everybody else?
- 9. Who needs the church?
- 10. Are heaven and hell real?

Now that you have some idea where this study is going, what would you say is a significant question of your own that you want answered in the weeks to come?

TAKE ACTION

God wants you to be part of His kingdom–to weave your story into His. That will mean change–to go His way rather than your own. This won't happen overnight, but it should happen steadily. By starting with small, simple choices, we begin to change our direction–with God's help along the way!

In this section, talk about how you will apply the wisdom you've learned from the teaching and Bible study. Then think about practical steps you can take in the coming week to live out what you've learned.

We all get stuck in our faith journey along the way. How might you go about getting "unstuck" based on today's conversation?

What's the one big thought you will take away from this session and how will you apply it to your life this week?

How will you interact with the Bible in the coming week? Share with the group how you plan to grow in your faith this week and then, at your next meeting, talk about your progress and challenges.

Ask, "How can we pray for you this week?" Invite everyone to share, but don't force the issue. Be sure to write prayer requests down in your notes section.

Close your meeting with prayer and talk specifics about your next group meeting.

FOR ADDITIONAL STUDY

If you feel God nudging you to go deeper, take some time before the next meeting to dig into His Word. Explore the Bible passages related to this session's theme on your own and jot your reflections in a journal or in this study guide. A great way to gain insight on a passage is to read it in several different translations. You may want to use a Bible app or website to compare translations.

Like Pastor Kevin mentioned, reading the book *"Grown Up Faith"* won't be identical to these sessions, but rather a reinforcement of the content. If you want to study further, read Chapters 1 & 2 of *"Grown Up Faith"*.

Therefore everyone who hears these words of mine and puts them into practice is like a wise man who built his house on the rock

(Matthew 7:24 NIV)

DAILY DEVOTIONALS

1

Psalm 119:105

Your word is a lamp for my feet, a light on my path (NIV).

Respond:
What two purposes for God's Word does this verse highlight?

2

Matthew 4:4

Jesus answered, "It is written: 'Man shall not live on bread alone, but on every word that comes from the mouth of God'" (NIV).

Respond:
Are you willing to "boast" of knowing the Lord in some way if God gives you that opportunity this next week? Have you asked Him to do so?

3

Matthew 7:24

Therefore everyone who hears these words of mine and puts them into practice is like a wise man who built his house on the rock (NIV).

Respond:
In what areas are you asking for God's help in connecting your "house" to the "rock" of His Word?

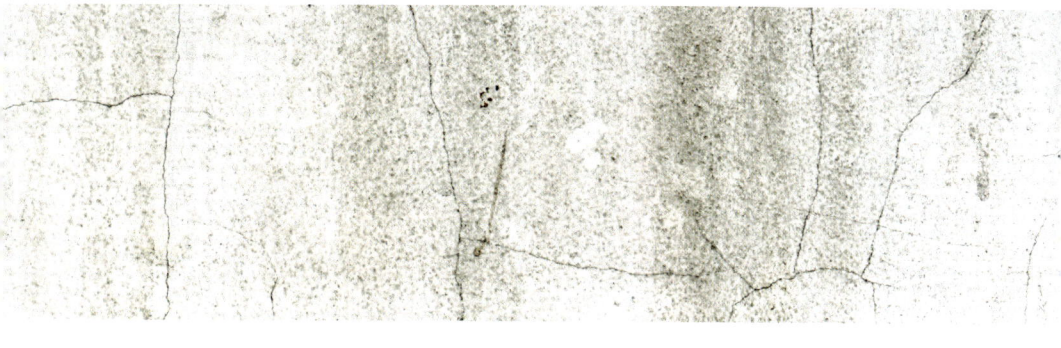

4

James 1:22

Do not merely listen to the word, and so deceive yourselves. Do what it says (NIV).

Respond:
What is this verse saying about the importance of going beyond reading or hearing God's Word? In what ways are you doing what it says?

5

Psalm 1:1-2

Blessed is the one who does not walk in step with the wicked or stand in the way that sinners take or sit in the company of mockers, but whose delight is in the law of the LORD, and who meditates on his law day and night (NIV).

Reflect:
The kind of meditation described in these verses requires a certain "uploading" or memorizing of God's Word. Consider the memory verse for this week again and experiment using it to meditate day and night. In what ways might you be blessed?

6

Use the following space to write any thoughts God has put in your heart and mind about the things we have looked at in this session and during your Daily Devotional time this week.

GOD'S BIGGER PICTURE

INTRODUCTION:

Last week, our conversation focused on establishing a strong faith foundation, which is necessary to building a grown-up faith. This foundation is secured by our ability to answer the "10 Core Questions of Life". But to answer them, we first need to understand God's bigger picture. Understanding the Bible's big picture not only reveals God's answers to life's core questions, but it gives our day-to-day life meaning, purpose, and direction. In other words, understanding God's bigger picture allows us to live bigger lives.

In this session, we want to take the next step and consider that God not only knows the answers we're looking for, but has actually given them to us in the Bible.

ICE-BREAKERS:

Describe a time when you misunderstood someone's words or actions because you didn't understand the whole context of the situation.

As the cliché statement declares, 'Don't judge a book by its cover.' Have you ever been guilty of falling into that trap?

For the benefit of those who may be joining us for the first time, let's take a few minutes to share what we learned in the last session. Share one insight you've been thinking about this week.

WEEKLY SCRIPTURE:

All Scripture is God-breathed and is useful for teaching, rebuking, correcting and training in righteousness, so that the servant of God may be thoroughly equipped for every good work. (2 Timothy 3:16-17)

This passage begins with the words "All Scripture" which underscores the idea that the entire Bible has a purpose. When we take the 10 core questions and line them up next to the Bible, we find something very interesting about the way scripture handles the most important questions people have. Let's jump into the conversation with Pastor Kevin as he helps us see the bigger picture of the Bible.

ᴍ *the bible binge podcast*

WATCH THE

VIDEO

SESSION 2

Use the notes space provided to record key thoughts, questions, and things you want to remember or follow up on. After watching the video, follow along with the questions and scriptures in the Group Discussion section.

The bible is

SEE THE BIBLICAL HISTORY ON PAGE 74.

GROUP DISCUSSION

First, take turns answering this question: What stood out to you the most from the teaching video?

Why is understanding the big picture of the Bible necessary to having a "grown-up" faith? What are the possible dangers in not understanding the big picture of the Bible?

During the Q&A portion of the video, Pastor Kevin encourages us to "lean into" the doubts because "doubt is partly how we come to faith." Why do you think doubt gives us an opportunity to grow in our faith?

Where in your Christian faith or the Bible do you most struggle with doubt? And what do you think it would look like to "lean into" those areas?

Pastor Kevin outlines the "10 Core Questions of Life" that make up our foundation:

1. Is life an accident or am I here on purpose?
2. Why do bad things happen to good people?
3. Can I really trust God?
4. Why can't I make my own rules?
5. Why can't God just accept me as I am?
6. Isn't one way to God narrow-minded?
7. What does it mean to be forgiven?
8. Why don't Christians look different from everybody else?
9. Who needs the church?
10. Are heaven and hell real?

Focus on the first question: Is life an accident or am I here on purpose? Discuss how the world tries to answer this without God. What are some of the problems with the world's answers to that question?

How would you answer that core question today? Is your life an accident or are you here on purpose?

How does knowing the "big picture" of the Bible help answer that question?

TAKE ACTION

In this section, talk about how you will apply the wisdom you've learned from the teaching and Bible study. Then think about practical steps you can take in the coming week to live out what you've learned.

The journey will come with its share of doubts and will require a greater level of faith. We shouldn't lean away from our doubts, but lean in, because our doubts allow God to give us a greater understanding of Himself and the life He's given us. This is the process for developing a grown-up faith.

Understanding God's bigger picture of the Bible and the impact for our lives takes time to develop.

Personally, how does seeing the "big picture" of the Bible change the way you will interact with scripture? How does it impact the way you see yourself and your life?

Which of the "10 Core Questions" have been significant hurdles in growing your faith? Where have you searched for answers outside of the Bible and how might today's session change how you respond to those doubts?

In what ways was the pyramid outline of the Bible and Pastor Kevin's brief explanations helpful to you? Which of these events are you least familiar with? What is your plan to increase your knowledge of this event?

Here are some simple ways to connect with God this week.
Tell the rest of the group which ones you plan to try this week, and talk about your progress and challenges when you meet next time.

Prayer. Commit to personal prayer and daily connection with God. You may find it helpful to write your prayers in a journal.

Daily Devotions. The Daily Devotions provided in each session offer an opportunity to read a short Bible passage five days a week during the course of our study. In our hurry-up world, we often move too quickly through everything—even reading God's Word! Slow down. Don't just skim, but take time to read carefully and reflect on the passage. Write down your insights on what you read each day. Copy a portion of scripture on a card and tape it somewhere in your line of sight, such as your car's dashboard or the bathroom mirror. Or, text it to yourself! Think about it when you sit at red lights or while you're eating a meal. Reflect on what God is saying to you through these words. On the sixth day, summarize what God has shown you throughout the week.

Ask, "How can we pray for you this week?" Invite everyone to share, but don't force the issue. Be sure to write prayer requests in your workbook.

Close your meeting with prayer.

FOR ADDITIONAL STUDY

If you feel God is nudging you to go deeper, take some time between now and our next meeting to dig into the Bible. Explore the Bible passages related to this session's theme on your own, jotting your reflections in a journal or in this workbook (suggestions would be Acts 17:16-24 and Romans 1:8-23). Also, if you haven't yet done so, pick up a copy of *"Grown Up Faith"* and read chapters 1 and 2 for additional study.

All Scripture is God-breathed and is useful for teaching, rebuking, correcting and training in righteousness, so that the servant of God may be thoroughly equipped for every good work.

(Matthew 7:24 NIV)

DAILY DEVOTIONALS

1

Hebrews 4:12

For the word of God is alive and active. Sharper than any double-edged sword, it penetrates even to dividing soul and spirit, joints and marrow; it judges the thoughts and attitudes of the heart (NIV).

Respond:
When was the last time you asked God to use His scalpel-like Word to work on your life?

2

2 Timothy 3:16-17

All Scripture is God-breathed and is useful for teaching, rebuking, correcting and training in righteousness, so that the servant of God may be thoroughly equipped for every good work (NIV).

Respond:
Meditate on examples for each of the four specific ways God uses His Word to impact our lives.

3

Psalm 119:9

How can a young person live a clean life? By carefully reading the map of your Word (MSG).

Respond:
Take a moment to review the "map" of God's Word/history you learned this week. Practice using your hands to remember the main events – this is a great tool for recalling God's bigger picture.

4

Acts 8:29-30

The Spirit told Philip, "Climb into the chariot." Running up alongside, Philip heard the eunuch reading Isaiah and asked, "Do you understand what you're reading?" (MSG).

Respond:
When was the last opportunity you had to speak to someone about God's Word? How would the outline of biblical history change the way you describe the flow of the Bible?

5

2 Timothy 3:16-17

All Scripture is God-breathed and is useful for teaching, rebuking, correcting and training in righteousness, so that the servant of God may be thoroughly equipped for every good work (NIV).

Respond:
Revisit this memory verse for the week. Consider what it means to be God-breathed and compare that to the creation of humans in Genesis 2. No wonder the Word is living! What are you doing this week with the objective of being more "thoroughly equipped" for what God wants to do in and through you?

6

Use the following space to write any thoughts God has put in your heart and mind about the things we have looked at in this session and during your Daily Devotional time this week.

3

IT'S TIME TO TRAIN

INTRODUCTION:

So far in these sessions we've been in a conversation about our personal transformation and journey to develop spiritual maturity – to have a grown-up faith. We've learned there are 10 core questions at the foundation of every person's faith, and we must answer them in one way or another. We've discovered that the Bible gives us answers to each of those questions. This is God's way of helping us establish a strong foundation and a biblical world-view for our lives. Now it's time to talk about the actual process of growing up in the faith in three distinct elements: the mind, the heart, and the will.

ICE-BREAKERS:

When you hear the word "training", what other words and life experiences come to mind?

What does the phrase "mind over matter" mean to you? Is that really possible?

Describe one way in which this study is already challenging the way you tend to look at life.

WEEKLY SCRIPTURE:

You've all been to the stadium and seen the athletes race. Everyone runs; one wins. Run to win. All good athletes train hard. They do it for a gold medal that tarnishes and fades. You're after one that's gold eternally.
(1 Corinthians 9:24-25 MSG)

The Bible, and in particular Jesus Himself, often uses ordinary events and the details of everyday life to illustrate spiritual principles. Day after day, our lives are filled with negative and positive lessons meant to teach and train us. Today's session will focus on the difference and the value of "training" over simply "trying." This distinction will help us better understand how God is forming us through even the smallest events in our lives, even those we would label as "bad."

WATCH THE

VIDEO

SESSION 3

Use the notes space provided to record key thoughts, questions, and things you want to remember or follow up on. After watching the video, follow along with the questions and scriptures in the Group Discussion section.

GROUP DISCUSSION

First, take turns answering this question: What stood out to you the most from the teaching video?

Early in this session, Pastor Kevin talks about "what went wrong" in the big picture of the Bible — Satan & Sin entered. How does that event still affect us in our day-to-day lives here and now?

How does Pastor Kevin's explanation of "why bad things happen to good people" help strengthen your foundation? What questions do you still have even after his answer?

Re-Read 1 Corinthians 9:24-27 (MSG):

"You've all been to the stadium and seen the athletes race. Everyone runs; one wins. Run to win. All good athletes train hard. They do it for a gold medal that tarnishes and fades. You're after one that's gold eternally."

In your own words, what would it look like to "win" in your faith? What is the relationship between training and winning?

What does this passage say about our prize for training in faith? How does knowing this encourage you and help you deal with the setbacks?

How do you respond to Pastor Kevin's challenge that we must train our minds with Biblical knowledge?

Read 2 Timothy 3:16-17 (MSG):

"Every part of Scripture is God breathed and useful one way or another—showing us truth, exposing our rebellion, correcting our mistakes, training us to live God's way. Through the Word we are put together and shaped up for the tasks God has for us."

This passage mentions that all scripture is useful for "training." As we grow up in our faith, we must look to God's Word as the tool to renew our minds. Without the truth of God's Word, sin allows lies into our thinking that eventually dulls our mind. This is where biblical training becomes vital to our spiritual maturity and helps us fight against the lies of Satan.

Romans 12 illustrates that our minds must be renewed in order to be transformed. What does it look like to have a mind renewed by scripture?

How have you seen the shift from Satan's lies to God's truth affect your own life? How does this train us to live God's way?

Pastor Kevin points out four other specific things the Bible provides to our lives as seen in the 2 Timothy passage. Can you point out all four and connect each point to how the Bible contributes to growing us up in the faith?

Why is "intentionality" important to a grown up faith? What tends to happen when our faith lacks intentionality in our daily rhythms and thinking?

TAKE ACTION

Remember, this section is all about the simple choices we can make daily to change the direction of our lives and grow up in our faith. Talk about how you will apply the wisdom you've learned today from the teaching and Bible study. Then, think about practical steps you can take in the coming week to live out what you've learned.

> What are some areas of life in which you can turn away from trying and intentionally approach things with training language and actions?

> Pastor Kevin mentioned that a grown-up faith is a "thinking faith." How can you exercise your faith by thinking more on Biblical truths rather than the lies of this world?

> How can you begin to allow scripture to renew your mind and move from information to transformation? What does a "disciplined life in God" look like practically, and how should it change you?

Challenge yourself this week to dive into scripture. As you read scripture this week, ask this question: "Besides showing me truth, how does this passage expose my rebellion, correct my mistakes, and/or train me to live God's way?"

Ask, "How can the rest of us pray for you this week?" Has one of the core questions or a comment during one of the session so far pushed a sensitive hot button you know you need prayer for?

Close your meeting with prayer.

FOR ADDITIONAL STUDY

Take some time between now and our next meeting to dig into God's Word. Explore the Bible passages related to this session's theme (suggestions would be Romans 12:1-2 and Joshua 1:7-9). Jot down your reflections in a journal or in this study guide. You may even want to use a Bible website or app to look up commentary on these passages. If you like, share what you learn with the group the next time you meet. Also, dive into Chapter 3 of *"Grown Up Faith"* for more study!

You've all been to the stadium and seen the athletes race. Everyone runs; one wins. Run to win. All good athletes train hard. They do it for a gold medal that tarnishes and fades. You're after one that's gold eternally

(1 Corinthians 9:24-25 MSG).

DAILY DEVOTIONALS

1

1 Timothy 4:7-8

Have nothing to do with godless myths and old wives' tales; rather, train yourself to be godly. For physical training is of some value, but godliness has value for all things, holding promise for both the present life and the life to come (NIV2011).

Respond:
What would be two or three significant habits that would be part of training yourself to be godly?

2

1 Corinthians 9:24-25

You've all been to the stadium and seen the athletes race. Everyone runs; one wins. Run to win. All good athletes train hard. They do it for a gold medal that tarnishes and fades. You're after one that's gold eternally (MSG).

Respond:
As you consider your current level of spiritual maturity, how have you progressed from where you were five years ago? Do these thoughts cause you to desire more maturity?

3

1 Timothy 4:15-16

Cultivate these things. Immerse yourself in them. The people will all see you mature right before their eyes! Keep a firm grasp on both your character and your teaching. Don't be diverted. Just keep at it. Both you and those who hear you will experience salvation (MSG).

Respond:
In many versions, the verb "mature" is the word "progress." How does training keep you from fixating on perfection in order to focus on moving forward, even when there are failures along the way?

4

Romans 12:1

So here's what I want you to do, God helping you: Take your everyday, ordinary life—your sleeping, eating, going-to-work, and walking-around life—and place it before God as an offering. Embracing what God does for you is the best thing you can do for him (MSG).

Respond:
It has often been said that the real problem with a living sacrifice is that it keeps crawling off the altar. What do you do when you discover that you've not been living as a living sacrifice?

5

1 Corinthians 10:13

No test or temptation that comes your way is beyond the course of what others have had to face. All you need to remember is that God will never let you down; he'll never let you be pushed past your limit; he'll always be there to help you come through it (MSG).

Reflect:
How does this verse help you deal with the failures and disappointments in your life-long experience of spiritual training under God's grace?

6

Use the following space to write any thoughts God has put in your heart and mind about the things we have looked at in this session and during your Daily Devotional time this week.

ENGAGING THE HEART

INTRODUCTION:

In the last session, we focused on training our minds by recognizing the usefulness of scripture to develop a grown-up faith. God's Word isn't just an inspiration—it is an application that should affect everything we do. Now, we're ready to tackle the next element of spiritual maturity— engaging our hearts to fully love and trust God.

ICE-BREAKERS:

After last week's session, what were some ways you intentionally trained your mind to think biblically this past week? Share any reflections or thoughts you had while reading the devotional passages.

Who in your life do you trust the most and why? Has that person changed over time? Why or why not?

What are some of the things that are road blocks for you or others when it comes to connecting with God on a more personal level?

WEEKLY SCRIPTURE:

God's Message: "Don't let the wise brag of their wisdom. Don't let heroes brag of their exploits. Don't let the rich brag of their riches. If you brag, brag of this and this only: That you understand and know me. I'm God, and I act in loyal love. I do what's right and set things right and fair, and delight in those who do the same things. These are my trademarks." God's Decree. (Jeremiah 9:23-24 MSG)

Knowing and understanding God is simple, yet complex. The key is that we relationally connect with Him, experiencing intimacy beyond just knowing about God. He doesn't want to just give us the answers to the "10 Core Questions of Life"; He wants to give us Himself and desires to build a relationship with us. A world-view based on a trusting, loving relationship with God is part of a grown-up faith. Let's join Pastor Kevin as we dive into a conversation about engaging our hearts.

WATCH THE

VIDEO

SESSION 4

Use the notes space provided to record key thoughts, questions, and things you want to remember or follow up on. After watching the video, follow along with the questions and scriptures in the Group Discussion section.

GROUP DISCUSSION

First, take turns answering this question: What stood out to you the most from the teaching video?

Engaging our hearts with God means we train ourselves to exercise a greater sense of trust. That largely means breaking from the temptation to take things into our own hands. It also means we let God speak to us through scripture, at the heart level. Intimacy and trust must be grown in us overtime, allowing us to experience the bigger life.

What are some areas of your life where you have an easy time trusting God? Why?

What are some areas of your life where you have a hard time trusting God?

Why is it often easy to trust yourself more than God?

Once we've settled that God can be trusted, more than ourselves, we must train our hearts to focus more on knowing God relationally, rather just knowing about God.

Share about a season or a time in your life where you felt distant from God. Was it a shortage of information or a shortage of relational intimacy?

Now, share about a season or a time where you felt close to God. Again, was it because of an abundance of information or an abundance of relational intimacy? What was the main difference in the two seasons?

Because we base our relationship with God like that of other human relationships, what are some things from our past experiences that keep us from knowing God more personally?

Re-Read Jeremiah 9:23-24 (MSG).

GOD's Message: "Don't let the wise brag of their wisdom. Don't let heroes brag of their exploits. Don't let the rich brag of their riches. If you brag, brag of this and this only: That you understand and know me. I'm GOD, and I act in loyal love. I do what's right and set things right and fair, and delight in those who do the same things. These are my trademarks." GOD's Decree.

What does it mean to "know and understand" God? Is that actually possible for us?

What is the evidence that someone is growing in heart-intimacy with God?

The town hall discussed the need to train our hearts to respond according to God's Word rather than our sensitivities. What did you take away from that conversation?

TAKE ACTION

In this section, talk about how you will apply the wisdom you've learned from the teaching and Bible study. Then, think about practical steps you can take in the coming week to live out what you've learned.

As we engage our hearts more with God, we learn that the answers to our questions aren't as important as simply having a closer relationship with Him. Spiritual maturity grows in us when, even in the midst of answers we may not like, we still love and trust God fully.

Like Abraham, how is waiting an exercise in trusting God? If you were Abraham, how would you have responded to God?

What are some areas of your life where you sense God is asking you to wait on Him? How can you practically engage your heart with Him in these seasons?

How can you use worship this week to help transition between knowing about God and knowing God more personally?

Some of us are more "thinkers" while others might call themselves more "feelers;" why is it crucial that we keep both mind and heart fully engaged as we relate to God and grow intimately with Him? How do we balance those?

Groups grow when they serve together. How could your group serve someone in need this week? You may want to provide a meal for a family who is going through difficulty, or give some other practical help to someone in need. If nothing comes to mind, spend some group time praying and asking God to show you who needs your help.

Ask, "How can the rest of us pray for you this week? Has one of the core questions or a comment during one of the session so far pushed a sensitive hot button you know you need prayer for?"

Close your meeting with prayer.

FOR ADDITIONAL STUDY

Take some time between now and our next meeting to dig into God's Word. Explore the Bible passages related to this session's theme on your own (suggestions would be Psalm 139 and John 21). Jot down your reflections in a journal or in this study guide. You may even want to use a Bible website or app to look up commentary on these passages. If you like, share what you learn with the group the next time you meet. Lastly, Chapter 4 of Grown Up Faith is a great resource and would give some additional illustrations and insights in the area of trusting God.

God's Message: "Don't let the wise brag of their wisdom. Don't let heroes brag of their exploits. Don't let the rich brag of their riches. If you brag, brag of this and this only: That you understand and know me. I'm God, and I act in loyal love. I do what's right and set things right and fair, and delight in those who do the same things. These are my trademarks."

(Jeremiah 9:23-24 MSG).

DAILY DEVOTIONALS

1

Proverbs 3:5-6

Trust in the Lord with all your heart and lean not on your own understanding; in all your ways submit to him, and he will make your paths straight (NIV).

Respond:
Which of the three choices to make recorded in this passage do you find most challenging? Why?

2

Jeremiah 9:23-24

This is what the Lord says: "Let not the wise boast of their wisdom or the strong boast of their strength or the rich boast of their riches, but let the one who boasts boast about this: that they have the understanding to know me, that I am the Lord, who exercises kindness, justice and righteousness on earth, for in these I delight," declares the Lord (NIV).

Respond:
Are you willing to "boast" of knowing the Lord in some way if God gives you that opportunity this next week? Have you asked Him to do so? How does God's Word compare to feeding yourself? Where can you improve?

3

2 Timothy 3:17.

Through the Word we are put together and shaped up for the tasks God has for us (MSG).

Respond:
Describe one way in which God's Word has shaped your attitudes, thinking, or emotional responses during this series.

4

Philippians 1:6

There has never been the slightest doubt in my mind that the God who started this great work in you would keep at it and bring it to a flourishing finish on the very day Christ Jesus appears (MSG).

Respond:
How could a verse like this help you put every day in perspective as you spend time alone with God at the end of it?

5

Philippians 3:8

What is more, I consider everything a loss because of the surpassing worth of knowing Christ Jesus my Lord, for whose sake I have lost all things. I consider them garbage, that I may gain Christ (NIV).

Reflect:
What are some things in your life that need to have a lower value attached to them so that you can more fully know Christ?

6

Use the following space to write any thoughts God has put in your heart and mind about the things we have looked at in this session and during your Daily Devotional time this week.

5

THE FREEDOM OF OBEDIENCE

INTRODUCTION:

There's something in all of us that resonates with freedom, but rebels against obedience. For that reason, let's pose a question: Can there really be freedom in obedience? Now that we've had conversations about training our minds and our hearts, we're ready to deal with the reality of our wills and the choices we make every day. We'll soon discover that it's not simply about living with or without rules; it's more about whose rules we choose to live by.

ICE-BREAKERS:

When you were young, what was the one "rule" in your household that you wished you could change, or the "rule" you constantly rebelled against?

What are some of the early lessons we learned ourselves, or that we teach our kids that can only be accomplished through the hardships of obedience?

WEEKLY SCRIPTURE:

If you hold to my teaching, you are really my disciples. Then you will know the truth, and the truth will set you free. (John 8:31-32)

There is freedom to be found inside of truth, but freedom only comes when we allow that truth to rule and have authority in our lives. As we journey through the three elements of spiritual maturity, you can see how all three must be at work to grow up in our faith. Loving God with our hearts and knowing the truths of scripture is incomplete. This knowledge and intimacy will leave us short of the bigger life unless we also surrender our will to His. As we also train in holy obedience, its then we can begin to experience the fullness of spiritual maturity at work in our lives.

WATCH THE

VIDEO

SESSION 5

Use the notes space provided to record key thoughts, questions, and things you want to remember or follow up on. After watching the video, work your way through the questions and scriptures in the Group Discussion section.

> Don't try harder,
> Seek words from
> your Father!
> *Open the bible*
> Transparency & accountability!

GROUP DISCUSSION

First, take turns answering this question: What stood out to you from the teaching video?

After watching the teaching, how would you answer the question we posed earlier: Can there really be freedom in obedience?

Do you struggle with listening to the rules set by others? How is it difficult for you to surrender your will [decisions] to those of someone else?

What do you think of when you consider someone/something having "authority" over you? What parallels can you draw from Pastor Kevin's story about his son trusting and obeying his instructions?

What would it take for you to give God full authority to speak into and direct your life? What is stopping you from getting to that place?

How can knowing God and knowing the bigger picture help you obey Him? Why is it so hard to obey someone without an established relationship of trust?

Read these passages in Matthew;

"Not everyone who calls me 'Lord, Lord' will enter the Kingdom of heaven, but only those who do what my Father in heaven wants them to do."
(Matthew 7:21).

"Our Father in heaven, hallowed be your name."

"Your kingdom come, your will be done, on earth as it is in heaven"
(Matthew 6:8, 10)

Why is it important to see Jesus' emphasis on obedience as a necessary part of our relationship with Him?

How does maturity form in us when we move beyond intimacy with Him and knowledge of His truth and put it into practice through obedience?

When we get serious about obeying Jesus, are we trying to earn something from Him, or are we trying to express something in response to what he has already done for us? Explain your choice.

Read Matthew 7:13-14 (MSG)

"Don't look for shortcuts to God. The market is flooded with surefire, easygoing formulas for a successful life that can be practiced in your spare time. Don't fall for that stuff, even though crowds of people do. The way to life—to God!—is vigorous and requires total attention.

Most of our immaturity in the arena of obedience can be traced to our responsiveness to anything that offers immediate gratification. Training towards a grown-up faith requires a different approach.

What are examples of ways we embrace short-term commitments and avoid discomfort and pain? Is this the way to spiritual maturity, why or why not?

TAKE ACTION

In this section, talk about how you will apply the wisdom you've learned from the teaching and Bible study. Then, think about practical steps you can take in the coming week to live out what you've learned.

How can you avoid the temptation to "make your own rules" this week?

How can you train this week in all three elements and ensure that your obedience doesn't become mechanical?

During his teaching Pastor Kevin said, "That is holy obedience. That's why believers who grow up in their faith strive to consistently follow Jesus' teachings on money, marriage, family, values, sexuality, relationships, business, and so on. Mature followers of Christ seek to be holy as He is holy. That requires obedience to Him."

How can you train in your ability to consistently follow Jesus' teachings when it comes to these topics? Is it knowledge or obedience that might be a next step towards greater maturity? Explain.

How would you explain holy obedience to someone who isn't here in this session? Moreover, how do we encourage fellow Christ-followers to train harder in obedience?

Since we have previously decided we won't say "I'll try to obey God," what are some points you've learned in this session that could serve you as training in obedience to Christ?

Spend some time praying about those you know who might need to hear about the insights you are learning during these sessions. Ask the Holy Spirit to bring to mind people you can pray for.

A step towards greater obedience may require accountability. Consider making a plan of action this week when it comes to simple obedience and ask a friend or spouse to encourage you and check-in. Then, at your next meeting, talk about your progress and challenges.

Close your meeting with prayer. Ask God to help clarify the solid lines and the boxes in the lives of those in your group.

FOR ADDITIONAL STUDY

Take some time between now and our next meeting to dig again into God's Word on your own. Explore the Bible passages related to this session's theme on your own (suggestions would be Genesis 3:1-24 and James 1:21-27). Jot down your reflections in a journal or in this study guide. You may even want to use a Bible website or app to look up commentary on these passages. If you like, share what you learn with the group the next time you meet. For more on obedience, read Chapter 5 of *"Grown Up Faith."*

If you hold to my teaching, you are really my disciples. Then you will know the truth, and the truth will set you free.

(John 8:31-32)

DAILY DEVOTIONALS

1

James 5:16

Make this your common practice: Confess your sins to each other and pray for each other so that you can live together whole and healed. The prayer of a person living right with God is something powerful to be reckoned with (MSG).

Respond:
Is there someone in your life you know you could confess sins to? Have you done that? If not, take a few moments to ask God to send someone like that into your life. And think about being that kind of person for someone else.

2

Philippians 2:13

That energy is God's energy, an energy deep within you, God himself willing and working at what will give him the most pleasure (MSG).

Respond:
What are some recent instances in which you know God was at work reinforcing your will to do His will rather than leaning toward your desires?

3

Matthew 7:21

Knowing the correct password–saying 'Master, Master,' for instance–isn't going to get you anywhere with me. What is required is serious obedience–doing what my Father wills (MSG).

Respond:
What does the balance between heart, mind, and will look like in your life right now in your relationship with God? Where are improvements needed?

4

James 1:25

But whoever catches a glimpse of the revealed counsel of God—the free life!—even out of the corner of his eye, and sticks with it, is no distracted scatterbrain but a man or woman of action. That person will find delight and affirmation in the action (MSG).

Respond:
In what ways is obeying God a life of genuine freedom?

5

Matthew 28:18-20

Jesus, undeterred, went right ahead and gave his charge: "God authorized and commanded me to commission you: Go out and train everyone you meet, far and near, in this way of life, marking them by baptism in the threefold name: Father, Son, and Holy Spirit. Then instruct them in the practice of all I have commanded you. I'll be with you as you do this, day after day after day, right up to the end of the age" (MSG).

Respond:
I low are you taking seriously the need to obey this command from Jesus as He was leaving earth?

6

Use the following space to write any thoughts God has put in your heart and mind about the things we have looked at in this session and during your Daily Devotional time this week.

LIVING GOD'S BIGGER LIFE

INTRODUCTION:

First, congratulations for making this journey with your group! Investing in this study will be a huge benefit towards growing up in your faith—but let's not forget what happens next. We can't simply internalize everything we've heard and conclude "We got this!" Everything we've learned has an external component. If we're really training towards transformation, others will take notice of the life change taking place in and through us. The unexpected result of drawing near to God is not only that He draws near to you, but that He also sends you out to live for Him in a world that still needs to know Him. Because the truth is, when we live with a world-view of the bigger picture, we live a bigger life for the things that last forever.

ICE-BREAKERS:

What has surprised you most about this group? Where did God challenge you most over the last few weeks?

What one idea, concept, or insight from this series do you think will still be shaping your thinking a year from now? Why?

Has this topic of eternity ever come up in conversations for you? How do you typically respond?

WEEKLY SCRIPTURE:

Jesus repeated his greeting: "Peace to you. Just as the Father sent me, I send you." (John 20:21 MSG)

As our study comes to an end, we need to emphasize that a grown-up faith is not a destination but a framework for engaging life. A grown-up faith never stops growing. In fact, learning to love God with all our hearts, souls, mind, and strength is not a process that will end this side of eternity, but will continue as we enter Heaven. That's the beauty of living according to God's bigger purpose – we get to partner with Him to play a role in His larger story – and that means more than just our time on earth. In the meantime, God has big plans for us, because His mission is bigger than we could ever dream. The point of developing spiritual maturity growing is that we might experience the greatest part of our bigger lives – being sent out into the world by our Heavenly Father, for His sake.

WATCH THE VIDEO

SESSION 6

Use the notes space provided to record any key thoughts, questions, and things you want to remember or follow up on. After watching the video, enjoy an extended conversation with the questions and scriptures provided in the Group Discussion section.

GROUP DISCUSSION

First, take turns answering this question: What stood out to you the most from the teaching video?

What was helpful about the review Pastor Kevin gave at the beginning of his teaching?

Which of these has been your greatest source of success; growing in your knowledge of God, growing in your intimacy with God, or growing in holy obedience to God?

What does the "hope of heaven" do for you as you seek to live a bigger life?

How would you answer the question posed by Pastor Kevin: "Are you living like Heaven is your home and earth is your hotel?" Explain.

Read Luke 15:25-32 (MSG).

All this time his older son was out in the field. When the day's work was done he came in. As he approached the house, he heard the music and dancing. Calling over one of the houseboys, he asked what was going on.
He told him, 'Your brother came home. Your father has ordered a feast—barbecued beef!—because he has him home safe and sound.'
The older brother stalked off in an angry sulk and refused to join in. His father came out and tried to talk to him, but he wouldn't listen. The son said, "Look how many years I've stayed here serving you, never giving you one moment of grief, but have you ever thrown a party for me and my friends? Then this son of yours who has thrown away your money on whores shows up and you go all out with a feast!"
His father said, "Son, you don't understand. You're with me all the time, and everything that is mine is yours—but this is a wonderful time, and we had to celebrate. This brother of yours was dead, and he's alive! He was lost, and he's found!' " (MSG)

The two sons show a contrast in how we interact and react to our Heavenly Father. How are they the same and how are they different?

What kind of people do each of the sons represent? What kind of relationship does the older son actually have with his father? Is it possible the older brother was a prodigal who stayed home but was just as lost as his little brother? Why or why not?

The core question in the background of this session is, "Are heaven and hell real?" How does eternity affect your engagement with those who are far from God (prodigals?). Should the reality of heaven/hell affect you? Why or why not?

Why would the celebration in the story take on greater meaning in light of the reality of eternity?

TAKE ACTION

As we begin to fully understand what it means to live a bigger life in light of God's bigger picture – we acknowledge our part. We are invited to join Jesus, to love people like Jesus loved people, and to tell others about Jesus. Wherever God has us on the map, we are on mission. Purposely placed to reach spiritually lost sons and daughters with His good news. We live with a world-view of the bigger picture and therefore we live a bigger life for the things that last forever.

How does the emphasis on a grown-up, matured, faith fit into your understanding of what it means to "live sent" in this world? How does "living sent" relate to God's promise of a bigger life within His bigger picture?

How do you respond to the challenge that genuine grown-up faith is not simply an unseen change in us, but always leads to the seen change through and around us? How would those around you say that this study has changed you?

In what ways does the reality of heaven and hell actually affect the way you treat others? If someone asked you that question (Are heaven and hell real?), how would you tackle that conversation?

We've mentioned mind, heart, and will throughout the series numerous times. How does each of these relate to "living sent" as a follower of Jesus?

What does it mean to "live on mission," and "live sent?" Would those who know you best use phrases like those to describe your life? Why or why not?

How can you begin to invest more in the kingdom of God and your local church?

How might the rest of the group pray for you regarding what you have learned during this series and the steps of training you sense God wanting you to practice going forward?

Close by praying for your prayer requests related to all you have learned. Spend some time thanking God for all He's done in your group during this study.

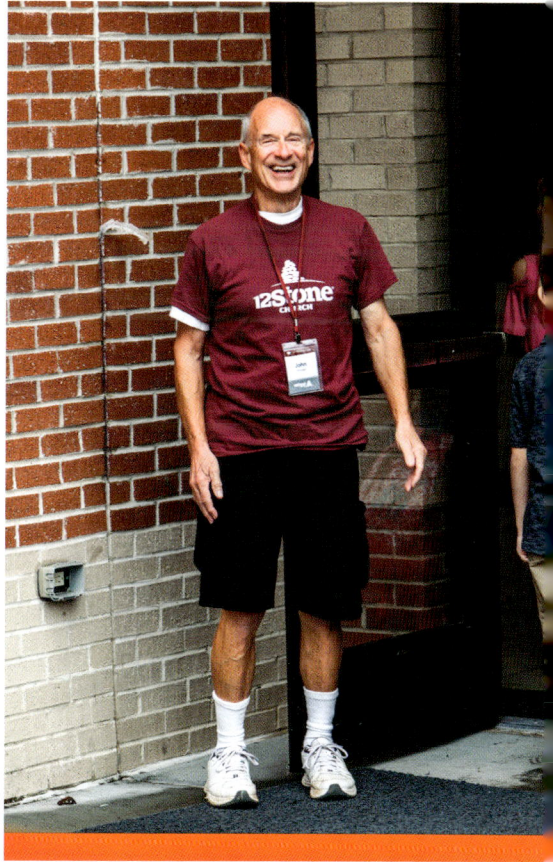

FOR ADDITIONAL STUDY

Explore the Bible passages related to this session's theme on your own, jotting your reflections in a journal or in this study guide (suggestions would be Romans 8:1-17 and Colossians 3:1-17). You may even want to use a Bible website or app to look up commentary on these passages.

Consider reading the book "*Grown Up Faith*" if you have not yet done so. Chapter 11 takes a closer look at the topic for this week's session.

Jesus repeated his greeting: "Peace to you. Just as the Father sent me, I send you."

(John 20:21 MSG).

DAILY DEVOTIONALS

1

Luke 19:10

"… For the Son of Man came to find and restore the (spiritually) lost."

Respond:
What did He have to do to find and restore you? Have you expressed your gratitude lately?

2

John 20:21

Jesus repeated his greeting: "Peace to you. Just as the Father sent me, I send you" (MSG).

Respond:
Write down three ways in which you are taking this command from Jesus seriously.

3

2 Peter 3:9

God isn't late with his promise as some measure lateness. He is restraining himself on account of you, holding back the End because he doesn't want anyone lost. He's giving everyone space and time to change (MSG)

Respond:
Make a list of at least ten people who you suspect have never surrendered their lives to Christ. Pray for each of them as the Holy Spirit reminds you and keep that list somewhere where you can underline it as you watch God work, even if He has to use you.

4

Hebrews 11:1

The fundamental fact of existence is that this trust in God, this faith, is the firm foundation under everything that makes life worth living. It's our handle on what we can't see (MSG).

Respond:
Describe the current level of growth in your faith. Let your mind, heart, and will speak into this description.

5

Micah 6:8

But he's already made it plain how to live, what to do, what GOD is looking for in men and women. It's quite simple: Do what is fair and just to your neighbor, be compassionate and loyal in your love, And don't take yourself too seriously– take God seriously (MSG).

Reflect:
How does this amazing verse give you hope for the future as you continue to pursue a grown-up faith?

6

Use the following space to write any thoughts God has put in your heart and mind about the things we have looked at in this session and during your Daily Devotional time this week.

MEMORY VERSES

SESSION ONE
Therefore everyone who hears these words of mine and puts them into practice is like a wise man who built his house on the rock. (Matthew 7:24 NIV)

SESSION TWO
All Scripture is God-breathed and is useful for teaching, rebuking, correcting and training in righteousness, so that the servant of God may be thoroughly equipped for every good work. (2 Timothy 3:16-17 NIV)

SESSION THREE
You've all been to the stadium and seen the athletes race. Everyone runs; one wins. Run to win. All good athletes train hard. They do it for a gold medal that tarnishes and fades. You're after one that's gold eternally. (1 Corinthians 9:24-25 MSG)

SESSION FOUR
Trust in the Lord with all your heart and lean not on your own understanding; in all your ways submit to him, and he will make your paths straight. (Proverbs 3:5-6 NIV)

SESSION FIVE
That energy is God's energy, an energy deep within you, God himself willing and working at what will give him the most pleasure. (Philippians 2:13 MSG)

SESSION SIX
Jesus repeated his greeting: "Peace to you. Just as the Father sent me, I send you". (John 20:21 MSG)

Jesus Christ
Matthew, Mark, Luke, John

The Old Covenant	**The New Covenant**
Genesis 12-Malachi	Acts - Jude
One World Government	**One World Government**
Genesis 10-11	Revelation 6-19
The World Judged and Destroyed	**The World Judged and Destroyed**
Genesis 6-9	Revelation 6-19
Satan and Sin Enter	**Satan and Sin Exit**
Genesis 305	Revelation 20
God and Righteous People in Paradise	**God and Redeemed People in Paradise**
Genesis 102	Revelation 20-22

NOTES